Baba Yaga

A Russian tale told by Martin Waddell

Illustrated by David Lopez

W
FRANKLIN WATTS
LONDON•SYDNEY

First published in 2009 by
Franklin Watts
338 Euston Road
London
NW1 3BH

Franklin Watts Australia
Level 17/207 Kent Street
Sydney
NSW 2000

A CIP catalogue record for this book is available
from the British Library.

ISBN 978 0 7496 8594 2 (hbk)
ISBN 978 0 7496 8600 0 (pbk)

Series Editor: Jackie Hamley
Series Advisor: Dr Barrie Wade
Series Designer: Peter Scoulding

Printed in China

Franklin Watts is a division of
Hachette Children's Books,
an Hachette UK company.
www.hachette.co.uk

This tale comes from
Russia. Can you find
Russia on a map?

Once there was a mean witch called Baba Yaga.

She lived in a magic
hut that walked about
on two legs like a hen.
A girl called Anya
came to the hut.

Anya heard a cat crying
and a dog whining
miserably. She opened
the creaky front door.

Anya fed the cat ...

gave the thin
dog a bone ...

and put oil on the
rusty door hinges.

7

Then Baba Yaga
caught Anya.

8

"Dinner!" Baba Yaga said, smacking her lips.

9

"Warn me if my dinner tries to escape!" Baba Yaga told her cat.

The cat hissed and
showed Anya her claws.
But ...

... the cat came to Anya when Baba Yaga had gone. "You fed me, so I will help you escape. You were kinder to me than Baba Yaga ever was," it purred.

"I know you won't squeak
and warn Baba Yaga!"
the cat told the door.

"Anya was kind to you and oiled your hinges."

15

The door opened

without a sound.

BABA YAGA

17

"I know you won't bark and warn Baba Yaga!" the cat told the dog.

"Anya was kind to you
and gave you a bone."

The dog wagged his tail
and let Anya pass.

"Who let my dinner escape?"

howled Baba Yaga.

The cat looked at the sky.
The dog stared up a tree.

The door slowly opened
and shut, without a creak.

And Baba Yaga ...

... got no dinner!

Puzzle 1

Put these pictures in the correct order.
Now tell the story in your own words.
What different endings can you think of?

Puzzle 2

kind   gentle

frightening

scary   horrid

generous

wicked   nasty

helpful

Choose the correct adjectives for each character. Which adjectives are incorrect? Turn over to find the answers.

Answers

Puzzle 1

The correct order is: 1c, 2e, 3f, 4b, 5d, 6a

Puzzle 2

Anya: the correct adjectives are gentle, kind

The incorrect adjective is frightening

Baba Yaga: the correct adjectives are horrid, scary

The incorrect adjective is generous

The cat: the correct adjective is helpful

The incorrect adjectives are nasty, wicked

Look out for Leapfrog fairy tales:

Cinderella
ISBN 978 0 7496 4228 0

The Three Little Pigs
ISBN 978 0 7496 4227 3

Jack and the Beanstalk
ISBN 978 0 7496 4229 7

The Three Billy Goats Gruff
ISBN 978 0 7496 4226 6

Goldilocks and the Three Bears
ISBN 978 0 7496 4225 9

Little Red Riding Hood
ISBN 978 0 7496 4224 2

Rapunzel
ISBN 978 0 7496 6159 5

Snow White
ISBN 978 0 7496 6161 8

The Emperor's New Clothes
ISBN 978 0 7496 6163 2

The Pied Piper of Hamelin
ISBN 978 0 7496 6164 9

Hansel and Gretel
ISBN 978 0 7496 6162 5

The Sleeping Beauty
ISBN 978 0 7496 6160 1

Rumpelstiltskin
ISBN 978 0 7496 6165 6

The Ugly Duckling
ISBN 978 0 7496 6166 3

Puss in Boots
ISBN 978 0 7496 6167 0

The Frog Prince
ISBN 978 0 7496 6168 7

The Princess and the Pea
ISBN 978 0 7496 6169 4

Dick Whittington
ISBN 978 0 7496 6170 0

The Little Match Girl
ISBN 978 0 7496 6582 1

The Elves and the Shoemaker
ISBN 978 0 7496 6581 4

The Little Mermaid
ISBN 978 0 7496 6583 8

The Little Red Hen
ISBN 978 0 7496 6585 2

The Nightingale
ISBN 978 0 7496 6586 9

Thumbelina
ISBN 978 0 7496 6587 6

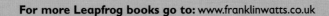

For more Leapfrog books go to: www.franklinwatts.co.uk